METUSELA ALBERT

LEARN HOW TO READ AND INTERPRET SCRIPTURE.

(THERE IS NO TRINITY GOD, IN HEAVEN).

To order additional copies of this book, contact:
Xlibris
844-714-8691
www.Xlibris.com
Orders@Xlibris.com

ISBN: Softcover   979-8-3694-3073-6
         EBook   979-8-3694-3074-3

Print information available on the last page

Rev. date: 09/24/2024

Contents

GENESIS 1:1 – In the beginning <u>God (ELOHIM)</u> created the heaven and the earth.

....
....
....
....

ISAIAH 43:10-11, 15.

v10. Ye are <u>my</u> witnesses, <u>saith the LORD</u>, and <u>my</u> servant whom <u>I</u> have choses: that ye may know and believe <u>me</u>, and understand <u>that I am he</u>: <u>before me there was no God formed, neither shall there be after me</u>

<u>v11</u>. <u>I, even I, am the LORD</u>; <u>and beside me there is no Savior.</u>

....
....
....
....

NOTE: ISAIAH 43:10-11, IS THE MAIN KEY TEXT THAT WILL CONDEMN THE TRINITY GOD THEORY.

GOD WAS TELLING PROPHET ISAIAH THAT HE ALONE WAS GOD, NONE BEFORE HIM, AND NONE AFTER HIM.

Dear Reader, take your time to read <u>the Singular Pronouns</u> mentioned in the given Scripture above.

The Pronoun - "My" was used 2 times.

The Pronoun - "I" was used 4 times.

The Pronoun – "Me" was used 4 times.

NOTE: THIS GOD WHO SPOKE TO PROPHET ISAIAH IN THE OLD

TESTAMENT ERA, WAS <u>NOT</u> A TRINITY GOD.

....
....
....
....

I often tell others, when you know the truth, you will easily know the error(s). But if you don't know the truth, then how on earth are you going to recognize the error(s)? You can't.

....
....
....
....

LET US LOOK AT ANOTHER POINT TO ESTABLISH THE TRUTH FURTHER. LET'S READ ISAIAH 43:15.

v15. I am the LORD, your Holy One, the creator of Israel, your King.

NOTE: THE GOD WHO SPOKE TO PROPHET ISAIAH WAS THE CREATOR, (ELOHIM).

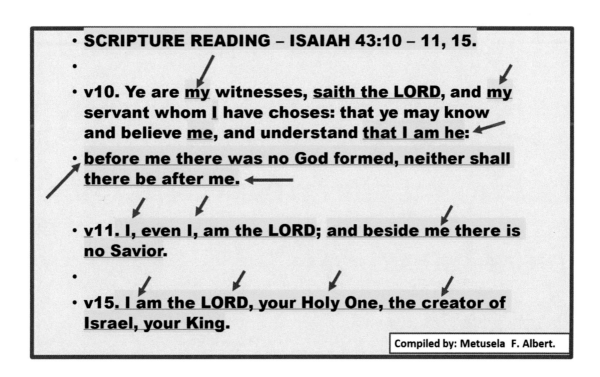

IT IS IMPORTANT THAT WE LEARN TO READ THE SINGULAR PRONOUNS ABOUT THE CONVERSATION BETWEEN GOD AND THE PROPHET ISAIAH. THE GOD WHO SPOKE TO PROPHET ISAIAH WAS "ELOHIM," THE CREATOR, OF HEAVEN AND EARTH. HE WAS THE LORD OF THE SABBATH – Genesis 1:1-31; & 2:1-3, Isaiah 43:15.

JESUS WAS THE LORD OF THE SABBATH – (Mark 2:27-28).

THEREFORE, THERE WAS NO SUCH THING AS GOD THE FATHER, AND THE SON (JESUS), CREATED HEAVEN AND EARTH. FURTHERMORE, THERE WAS NO SUCH THING AS, GOD THE FATHER, GOD THE SON, AND GOD THE HOLY SPIRIT, CREATED

HEAVEN AND EARTH IN SIX DAYS AND RESTED ON THE SEVENTH DAY.

NOTE: ELOHIM, THE CREATOR, WHO SPOKE TO PROPHET ISAIAH WAS <u>NOT</u> A TRINITY GOD – (Isaiah 43:15).

JESUS WAS <u>NOT</u> A TRINITY GOD.

THUS, JESUS WHO WAS "<u>ELOHIM</u>," <u>DID NOT HAVE</u> A BEGOTTEN SON CALLED – JESUS.

JESUS, WHO WAS THE FATHER OF THE CHILDREN OF ISRAEL, DID <u>NOT</u> SEND <u>A SON</u> CALLED – "JESUS, TO DIE AT CALVARY.

THE TRUTH IS:

JESUS, WHO WAS THE FATHER, TOOK HUMAN FLESH BY INCARNATION THROUGH MARY AT BETHLEHEM, AND BECAME THE SON. HE VOLUNTARILY DIED AT CALVARY, TO PAY FOR THE PENALTY OF SIN, AS IF HE WAS A SINNER. THIS IS THE MOST AMAZING LOVE OF GOD.

GOD THE FATHER <u>BECAME THE SON</u> BY THE INCARNATION PROCESS. GOD DID <u>NOT</u> SEND A SON. IN FACT, GOD DID <u>NOT</u> HAVE A BEGOTTEN SON.

....
....
....
....

IF CHRISTIANITY HAD UNDERSTOOD <u>THE INCARNATION DOCTRINE</u>, SURELY, THEY WOULD NOT HAVE BELIEVED IN THE FALSE TRINITY GOD THEORY, THAT SAYS, THREE PERSONS IN ONE GOD.

THE TRINITY GOD EQUATION THAT SAYS, <u>THREE IN ONE</u>, IS SATANIC.

$1 + 1 + 1 = 1$ GOD, IS DEVILISH.

I repeat: GOD the Father + GOD the Son + GOD the Holy Spirit = 1 GOD, IS INSANE.

....
....
....
....

THE TRUTH IS: JESUS, WAS AND IS, AN ETERNAL GOD. HE WAS THE FIRST, AND THE LAST. HE DOES <u>NOT</u> NEED TO BE COMBINED WITH ANOTHER TWO BEINGS, TO MAKE ONE GOD. HE WAS SELF-EXISTENT.

....
....
....
....

AGAIN, IF CHRISTIANITY HAD UNDERSTOOD WHAT GOD SAID TO PROPHET ISAIAH IN CHAPTER 43:10-11, HENCE, THEY WOULD NOT HAVE FALLEN INTO THE LIES OF A TRINITY GOD THEORY.

....
....
....
....

WE MUST CONFRONT, CONDEMN, AND REBUKE, THE FALSE TRINITY GOD THEORY, THAT DECEIVED MILLIONS OF PEOPLE FOR DECADES.

The Trinity GOD concept has demoted JESUS from being a self-existent GOD, to a Son of GOD, with a beginning; either he was born by GOD the FATHER, OR was created by him, before the angels existed.

....
....
....
....

It is better for us to offend our earthly friends and others by telling the truth that there was no Trinity GOD, than to offend JESUS, our only ELOHIM, who created us in his image. Amen? Yes!

....
....
....
....

HERE IS THE THING: I CHOSE NOT TO BELIEVE IN THE FALSE TRINITY GOD THEORY.

THAT IS THE REASON THIS BOOK WAS CREATED TO HELP THOSE WHO DID <u>NOT</u> KNOW WHO JESUS WAS, AND IS.

LEARN HOW TO READ AND INTERPRET SCRIPTURE IN <u>THE CONTEXT</u> AND <u>CHRONOLOGICAL ORDER.</u> <u>BEGIN READING THE SCRIPTURES FROM GENESIS</u> <u>CHAPTER 1:1-31 AND 2:1-3.</u>

....

....

....

....

INTRODUCTION

Genesis 1:26 is the first Scripture that is being misinterpreted by most Churches and Pastors, to justify the Trinity God theory. Someone had asked me at one time, where should we begin reading the Bible? I answered, I recommend that we begin with Genesis Chapter 1:1-31. Start from the beginning to avoid misinterpreting the Scriptures. Learn to read the Context of Genesis Chapter 1:1-31. Look for Pronouns that represent GOD.

NOTE: Don't start reading the Bible from the New Testament nor in John 3:16. If you need to memorize a Text about our only GOD, go to Isaiah 43:10-11. In the POWER POINT SLIDE below, is an example of reading the Pronouns in Genesis 1:5, 10, 16.

YOU can't understand Genesis 1:26, unless you first understand the SINGULAR PRONOUNS used in Genesis 1:5, 10, 16. In those three verses, the PRONOUNS used for GOD, are "HE." That is the IMMEDIATE CONTEXT before Genesis 1:26.

HOW TO READ SCRIPTURE IN THE CONTEXT

- Genesis 1:1-5 (King James Version)

- **1.** In the beginning **God** created the heaven and the earth.

- ² And the earth was without form and void, and darkness was upon the face of the deep. And **the Spirit of God** moved upon the face of the waters.

- ³ And **God said**, "Let there be light"; and there was light.

- ⁴ And **God** saw the light, that it was good; and God divided the light from the darkness.

NOTE: THE PRONOUN USED IN VERSE 5 = "HE," NOT "THEY."

- ⁵ And **God** called the light Day, and the darkness **He** called Night. And the evening and the morning were the first day.

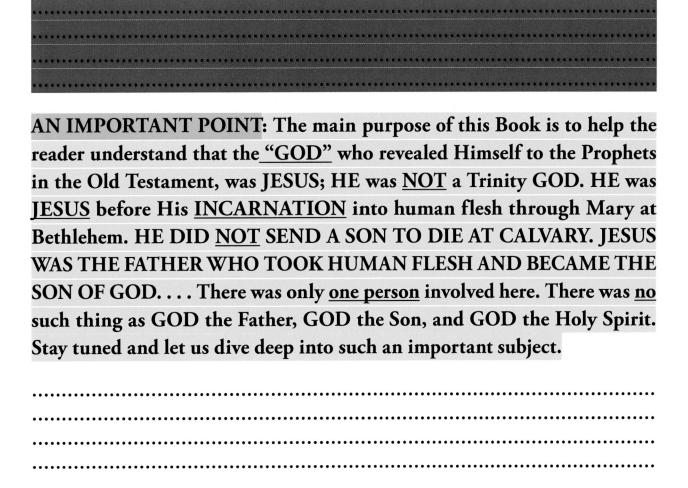

AN IMPORTANT POINT: The main purpose of this Book is to help the reader understand that the "GOD" who revealed Himself to the Prophets in the Old Testament, was JESUS; HE was NOT a Trinity GOD. HE was JESUS before His INCARNATION into human flesh through Mary at Bethlehem. HE DID NOT SEND A SON TO DIE AT CALVARY. JESUS WAS THE FATHER WHO TOOK HUMAN FLESH AND BECAME THE SON OF GOD. . . . There was only one person involved here. There was no such thing as GOD the Father, GOD the Son, and GOD the Holy Spirit. Stay tuned and let us dive deep into such an important subject.

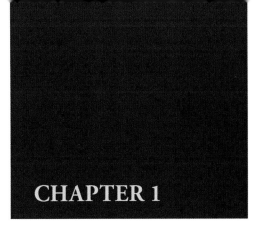

CHAPTER 1

READ THE <u>CONTEXT</u> IN A <u>CHRONOLOGICAL ORDER</u>.

> **READ THE PRONOUNS IN GENESIS 1:5, 10, 16 = "HE".**
>
> - **Genesis 1:1, 5, 10, 16.**
> - **v1. In the beginning <u>God</u> created the heaven and the earth.**
>
> - **v5. And <u>God</u> called the light Day, and the darkness <u>he</u> called Night. And the evening and the morning were the first day.**
>
> - **v10. And <u>God</u> called the dry land Earth; and the gathering together of the waters called <u>he</u> Seas: and <u>God</u> saw that it was good.**
>
> - **v16. And <u>God</u> made two great lights; the greater light to rule the day, and the lesser light to rule the night: <u>he</u> made the stars also.**
>
> Compiled by: Metusela F. Albert.

I hope you can see <u>the Singular Pronouns</u> in those three verses before reading Genesis 1:26.

....
....
....
....

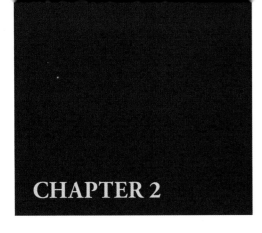

CHAPTER 2

PRECEPT UPON PRECEPT. READ - EXODUS 3:13-14; JOHN 5:39, 46-47; 8:56-58. THIS IS ABOUT "THE WIDER CONTEXT". SCRIPTURE INTERPRETS ITSELF.

First, Let's Read - Exodus 3:13-14.

v13. And Moses said unto God, Behold, and when I come unto the children of Israel, and shall say unto them, The God of your fathers hath sent me unto you; and they shall say to me, What is his name? What shall I say unto them?

v14. And God said unto Moses, I AM THAT I AM: and he said: Thus shalt say unto the children of Israel, I AM hath send me unto you.

....
....
....
....

WHO WAS THE GOD CALLED "I AM THAT I AM," WHO SPOKE TO MOSES AT THE BURNING BUSH?

Let's Read John 5:39 and 5:46. Allow JESUS to EXPLAIN IT.

In John 5:39, JESUS said, "Search the Scriptures; for in them ye think ye have eternal life: and they are <u>they which testify</u> <u>of me.</u>"

<u>In John 5:46, JESUS said, For had ye believed Moses, ye</u> <u>would have believed me: for he wrote of me.</u>

<u>v47. But if ye believe not his writings, how shall ye believe my</u> <u>words? Jesus answered, Ye neither know me, nor my Father,</u> <u>if ye had known me, ye should have known my Father also.</u>

Let us read - John 8:12-14, 18-19; AND 8:56-59.

V12 – Jesus said unto them, saying, <u>I am the light of the</u> <u>world</u>: he that followeth <u>me</u> shall not walk in darkness, but shall have the light of life.

V13 – The Pharisees therefore, said unto him, Thou barest record of thyself; thy record is not true.

V14 – Jesus answered and said unto them, Though I bear record of <u>myself</u>, yet <u>my record</u> is true; <u>for I know whence I</u> <u>came, and whither I go</u>; but ye cannot tell whence I come, and whither I go.

V18 – <u>I am One that bear witness of myself</u>, and <u>the Father</u> that sent me barest witness of <u>me.</u>

V19 – Then said they unto him, <u>where is thy Father</u>?

....
....
....
....

v56 – Your Father Abraham rejoiced to see my day: and he saw it, and was glad.

v57 – Then said the Jews unto him, Thou art not yet fifty years old, and hast thou seen Abraham?

v58 – Jesus said unto them, Verily, verily, I say unto you, Before Abraham was, I am.

V59 – Then took they up stones to cast at him: but Jesus hid himself, and went out of the temple, going through the midst of them, and so passed by.

....
....
....
....

THE POINT IS:

1. JESUS is the light of the world. HE was the ELOHIM who created the light in Genesis 1:3.
2. JESUS existed before Abraham.
3. THE TWO NATURES IN JESUS. ((Please pay careful attention to this crucial point)).

WE NEED TO UNDERSTAND THE TWO NATURES, THE DIVINE NATURE AND THE HUMAN NATURE, IN JESUS WHILE HE WAS IN HUMAN FLESH.

JESUS, BEING THE GOD OF ABRAHAM, HAD ONLY A DIVINE NATURE BEFORE THE INCARNATION AT BETHLEHEM THROUGH MARY.

HE CANNOT DIE AT CALVARY TO BECOME THE SIN OFFERING, IF HE DID NOT TAKE UP HUMAN NATURE THROUGH MARY. . . . BEING GOD, HE CANNOT DIE.THAT IS THE REASON HE TOOK UP THE INCARNATION PROCESS THROUGH MARY AT BETHLEHEM, TO ENABLE HIM TO DIE, TO PAY THE PENALTY OF SIN, YET NEVER SINNED.

ANOTHER REASON HE TOOK UP HUMAN NATURE, IS TO PROVE THAT THE LAW CAN BE KEPT BY HUMAN BEINGS WHO ARE BORN WITH A FALLEN SINFUL NATURE. IF YOU REMEMBER, JESUS SAID, IF YOU LOVE ME, KEEP MY COMMANDMENTS – John 14:15. YES, THE COMMANDMENTS CAN BE KEPT BY THOSE WHO ABIDE IN JESUS CHRIST – (1 JOHN 3:4-9; Revelation 22:11-14).

WHEN JESUS INCARNATED INTO HUMAN FLESH THROUGH MARY AT BETHLEHEM TO PAY FOR THE PENALTY OF SIN, HE TOOK UPON HIMSELF A HUMAN NATURE. IN HUMANITY, JESUS DID NOT CEASE FROM BEING DIVINE. BUT HE VEILED HIS DIVINE NATURE. AND THE JEWS ONLY SAW HIM AS ANOTHER PROPHET LIKE MOSES, ELIJAH, ISAIAH, JEREMIAH, ETC.

SO, WHEN JESUS WAS IN HUMAN FLESH, THE JEWS DID NOT KNOW THAT HE WAS THE GOD OF ABRAHAM, THE FATHER OF THE CHILDREN OF ISRAEL. EVEN JOHN AND PAUL DID NOT KNOW THAT JESUS WAS THE GOD OF ABRAHAM, ISAAC, AND JACOB, WHO CAME IN HUMAN FLESH.

THEREFORE, WHEN YOU READ THE CONVESATION OF JESUS WITH THE PHARISEES IN THE SCRIPTURES ABOVE, HE WAS TRYING TO OPEN THEIR EYES TO RECOGNIZE HIM AS THE GOD OF ABRAHAM WHO CAME IN HUMAN FLESH, AS PROPHESIED IN ISAIAH 9:6; 7:14; ISAIAH 44:24; 49:16. JESUS TALKED OF HIS FATHER IN HEAVEN, AS IF HE WAS A DIFFERENT PERSON FROM HIM, YET HE WAS THE SAME PERSON. TRY AND READ JOHN 14:6-9, THE CONVERSATION BY THOMAS, PHILIP, AND JESUS, IN REFERENCE TO THE FATHER.

....
....
....
....

REVELATION 21:5-7.

PLEASE READ WHAT GOD SAID TO JOHN ON THE ISLAND OF PATMOS. HE WAS JESUS, THE ALPHA AND OMEGA.

THE DISCIPLE JOHN LAST HEARD OF THE PHRASE – "IT IS DONE," AT CALVARY (31 A.D.) WHEN JESUS WAS ABOUT TO DIE ON THE CROSS. NOW, WHILE JOHN WAS PERSECUTED AND ISOLATED ON THE ISLAND OF PATMOS, JESUS CAME AND SPOKE TO HIM PERSONALLY, TO ENCOURAGE HIM. JESUS REMINDED JOHN THAT HE WAS THE GOD OF PROPHET ISAIAH THAT WAS WRITTEN, IN ISAIAH 43:10-11, 44:6, 24. HE WAS THE MESSIAH WHO SPOKE TO THE SAMARITAN WOMAN AT JACOB'S WELL. HE WAS CRUCIFIED AT CALVARY BY THE ROMAN SOLDIERS – 31 A.D. HE WAS RESURRECTED AND IS ALIVE FOREVERMORE. . . . HE IS COMING BACK AGAIN, AS PROMISED – John 14:1-3.

THE DISCIPLE JOHN KNEW JESUS AS THE SON OF MARY AND JOSEPH FROM NAZARETH. . . JOHN HAD NOT KNOWN THAT JESUS WAS THE GOD OF PROPHET ISAIAH, THE CREATOR, OF HEAVEN AND EARTH. JESUS BECAME A PERSONAL GOD TO JOHN ON THE ISLAND OF PATMOS. JOHN WAS GIVEN A REVELATION TO WRITE THE BOOK OF REVELATION BEFORE HIS DEATH.

THE BOOK OF REVELATION WAS WRITTEN BY JOHN AROUND 95 A.D. OR 96 A.D. WOW! THIS SCRIPTURE IS SO UPLIFTING TO LEARN OF THE TRUE GOD CALLED – "ALPHA AND OMEGA", WHO SITS ON THE THRONE. DEATH IS IMMINENT TO JOHN, BUT JESUS REASSURED JOHN OF LIFE AFTER DEATH. THE JESUS THAT JOHN KNEW AS THE SON OF MARY AND JOSEPH, WILL BECOME HIS GOD. HE WAS THE GOD SITTING ON THE THRONE. WOW! WHAT A TESTIMONY TO PERSONALLY HEAR WHAT JESUS SAID TO JOHN ON THE ISLAND OF PATMOS.

READ THE SINGULAR PRONOUNS. JESUS WAS NOT A TRINITY GOD.

....
....
....
....

- **Revelation 21:5-7 - King James Version**

- **⁵ And he that sat upon the throne said,**

- **Behold, I make all things new. And he said unto me, Write: for these words are true and faithful.**

- **⁶ And he said unto me, It is done. I am Alpha and Omega, the beginning and the end. I will give unto him that is athirst of the fountain of the water of life freely.**

- **⁷ He that overcometh shall inherit all things; and I will be his God, and he shall be my son.**

Compiled by: Metusela F. Albert.

....
....
....
....

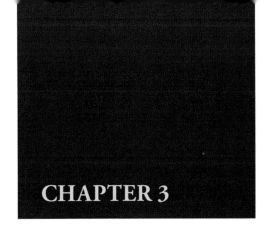

CHAPTER 3

JESUS WAS THE "ELOHIM" WHO CREATED HEAVEN AND EARTH. GENESIS 1:1.

HE WAS THE "ELOHIM" WHOM MOSES WROTE IN THE FIRST FIVE BOOKS OF THE HEBREW BIBLE CALLED – THE TORAH.

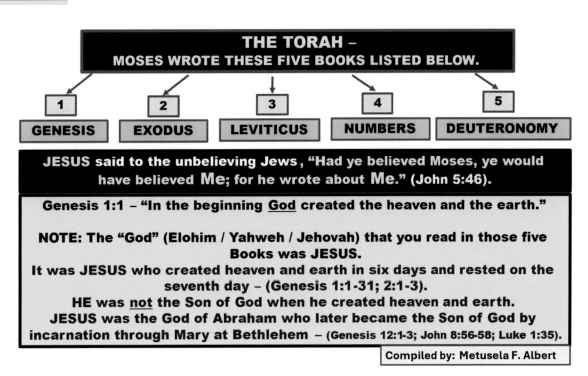

THE TORAH –
MOSES WROTE THESE FIVE BOOKS LISTED BELOW.

1	2	3	4	5
GENESIS	EXODUS	LEVITICUS	NUMBERS	DEUTERONOMY

JESUS said to the unbelieving Jews, "Had ye believed Moses, ye would have believed Me; for he wrote about Me." (John 5:46).

Genesis 1:1 – "In the beginning God created the heaven and the earth."

NOTE: The "God" (Elohim / Yahweh / Jehovah) that you read in those five Books was JESUS.
It was JESUS who created heaven and earth in six days and rested on the seventh day – (Genesis 1:1-31; 2:1-3).
HE was not the Son of God when he created heaven and earth.
JESUS was the God of Abraham who later became the Son of God by incarnation through Mary at Bethlehem – (Genesis 12:1-3; John 8:56-58; Luke 1:35).

Compiled by: Metusela F. Albert

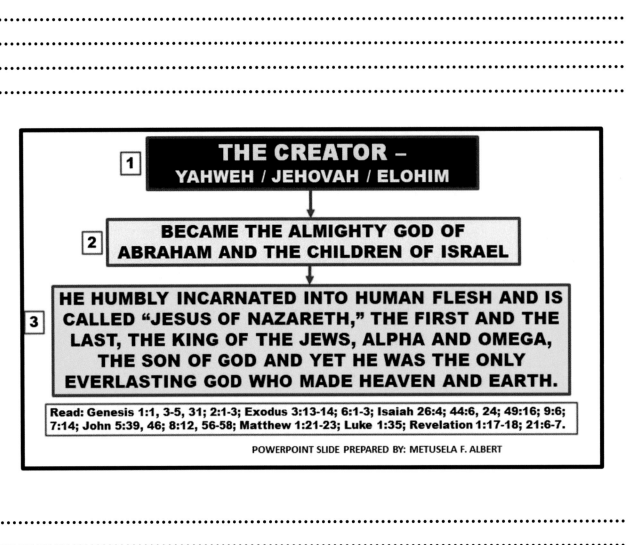

CHAPTER 4

GENESIS 1:5,10, 16 – PRONOUNS USED ARE "HE", NOT "THEY".

Most people failed to read and understand these three verses which are the context to the ELOHIM that you read in Genesis 1:1. The SINGULAR PRONOUNS used in these three verses are the CONTEXT which tells of the "ELOHIM" who created heaven and earth in six days and rested on the seventh day.

"HE," NOT "THEY."

Therefore, the "ELOHIM" who created heaven and earth was NOT a TRINITY GOD. These three Scriptures mut be understood *before* reading Genesis 1:26.

Well, let's read the three Scriptures mentioned so that you can understand the point I am sharing.

....
....
....
....

Genesis 1: 5, 10, 16.

v5. And God called the light Day, and the Darkness he called Night. And the evening and the morning were the first day.

v10. And <u>God</u> called the dry land Earth; and the gathering together of the waters <u>he</u> called Seas: and <u>God</u> saw that it was good.

v16. And <u>God</u> made two great lights; the greater light to rule the day, and the lesser light to rule the night: <u>he</u> made the stars also,

///
///
///
///

HOW TO READ SCRIPTURE IN THE CONTEXT

Compiled by : Metusela F. Albert

- Genesis 1:1-5 (King James Version)
- **1.** In the beginning <u>God</u> created the heaven and the earth.
- ² And the earth was without form and void, and darkness was upon the face of the deep. And **the Spirit of God** moved upon the face of the waters.
- ³ And <u>God said</u>, "Let there be light"; and there was light.
- ⁴ And <u>God</u> saw the light, that it was good; and God divided the light from the darkness.

NOTE: THE PRONOUN USED IN VERSE 5 = "HE," NOT "THEY."

- ⁵ And <u>God</u> called the light Day, and the darkness <u>He</u> called Night. And the evening and the morning were the first day.

Compiled by : Metusela F. Albert

Compiled by : Metusela F. Albert

Compiled by : Metusela F. Albert

NOTE: Many people may have read numerous times those three verses mentioned above, but did <u>not</u> understand the point I am sharing in here; and that is why they are still believing in the <u>False Trinity GOD</u> theory. THEY FAILED TO UNDERSTAND <u>THE IMMEDIATE CONTEXT</u>.

READ THE PRONOUNS IN GENESIS 1:5, 10, 16 = "HE

- Genesis 1:1, 5, 10, 16.

- v1. In the beginning **God** created the heaven and the earth.

- v5. And **God** called the light Day, and the darkness **he** called Night. And the evening and the morning were the first day.

- v10. And **God** called the dry land Earth; and the gathering together of the waters called **he** Seas: and **God** saw that it was good.

- v16. And **God** made two great lights; the greater light to rule the day andthe lesser light to rule the night: **he** made the stars also.

Compiled by: Metusela F. Albert.

Dear Reader, before you read any further from here, just want to remind you that you need to understand the point shared above. If you haven't grasped the point, please go back and re-read until you fully understand the point above. Thank you.

....

....

....

....

HOW TO READ THE <u>CONTEXT</u> AND UNDERSTAND SCRIPTURE.

- **THE FIRST MISINTERPRETED SCRIPTURE TO JUSTIFY THE TRINITY GOD THEORY IS - GENESIS 1:26.**

- NOTE: MOST PEOPLE DO NOT READ <u>THE CONTEXT</u> IN:
- Genesis 1:1. (GOD CREATED HEAVEN AND EARTH).
- Genesis 1:5. (THE PRONOUN IS– "HE."
- Genesis 1:10. (THE PRONOU IS– "HE."
- Genesis 1:16. (THE PRONOUN IS– "HE."
- Genesis 1:27-31. (THE PRONOUN IS– "HE."
- Genesis 2:1-3. (THE PRONOUN IS– "HE" and "HIS".

Compiled by: Metusela F. Albert.

....
....
....
....

CHAPTER 5

HOW TO INTERPRET GENESIS 1:26 - 31; AND 2:1-3.

Let's read Genesis 1:26-31.

²⁶ And God said, Let us make man in our image, after our likeness: and let them have dominion over the fish of the sea, and over the fowl of the air, and over the cattle, and over all the earth, and over every creeping thing that creepeth upon the earth.

²⁷ So God created man in his own image, in the image of God created he him; male and female created he them.

²⁸ And God blessed them, and God said unto them, Be fruitful, and multiply, and replenish the earth, and subdue it: and have dominion over the fish of the sea, and over the fowl of the air, and over every living thing that moveth upon the earth.

²⁹ And God said, Behold, I have given you every herb bearing seed, which is upon the face of all the earth, and every tree,

in the which is the fruit of a tree yielding seed; to you it shall be for meat.

³⁰ And to every beast of the earth, and to every fowl of the air, and to every thing that creepeth upon the earth, wherein there is life, I have given every green herb for meat: and it was so.

³¹ And God saw every thing that he had made, and, behold, it was very good. And the evening and the morning were the sixth day.

....
....
....
....

According to Genesis 1: 26, GOD (ELOHIM) was talking to someone who had the same nature, as GOD. We must find out who was that person that GOD was talking to, that had that same IMAGE.

Question # 1 – WHO WAS GOD (ELOHIM) TALKING TO, IN VERSE, 26?

Question # 2 – WHAT IS GOD'S (ELOHIM'S) IMAGE?

Question # 3 – WHAT IS THE IMMEDIATE CONTEXT, in verses 27-31?

Question # 4 – WHAT IS THE IMMEDIATE CONTEXT, in Genesis 2:1-3?

Do you still Remember? – The IMMEDIATE CONTEXT before Genesis 1:26, is found in these three verses - Genesis 1:5, 10, 16. – Three Singular Pronouns used – "HE." I assume you have read CHAPTER 2, regarding this valid Point.

....
....
....
....

It was obvious that GOD was talking to someone who had the same "IMAGE," as GOD.

""
""
""
""

POINT

 # 1 – GOD'S IMAGE IS SINLESSNESS.

 # 2 – GOD WAS GOING TO CREATE ADAM AND EVE AS SINLESS BEINGS.

 # 3 – THE ANGELS IN HEAVEN WERE CREATED SINLESS.

 # 4 – WHEN LUCIFER AND ONE THIRD OF THE ANGELS DISOBEYED GOD, THEY NO LONGER HAVE GOD'S IMAGE. THUS, THEY WERE CAST OUT OF HEAVEN TO OUR PLANET EARTH.

5. WAS GOD TALKING TO THE UNFALLEN ANGELS WHO STILL HAVE GOD'S SINLESS IMAGE? WE DON'T KNOW.

6. WAS GOD TALKING TO HIS SON WHO EXISTED BEFORE THE ANGELS WERE CREATED? NO! . . . . GOD DID NOT HAVE A BEGOTTEN SON, IN HEAVEN, BEFORE THE ANGELS WERE CREATED.

7. IS IT POSSIBLE THAT GOD WAS TALKING TO ANGEL GABRIEL? POSSIBLY. . . . . ANGEL GABRIEL WAS THE ANGEL THAT SPOKE TO ZACHARIAH AND ELIZABETH, THE PARENTS OF JOHN THE BAPTIST.

8. ANGEL GABRIEL WAS THE ANGEL THAT SPOKE TO MARY AND INFORMED HER OF HER PREGNANCY BY THE POWER OF THE HOLY SPIRIT.

9. ANGEL GABRIEL DID NOT CREATE ADAM AND EVE. GENESIS 1:27-31.

#10. JESUS WAS THE "ELOHIM" WHO CREATED ADAM AND EVE, AND EVERYTHING AS RECORED IN GENESIS 1:1-31.

#11. JESUS WAS THE LORD OF THE SABBATH DAY – GENESIS 2:1-3.

#12. THERE WAS NO SUCH THING AS A TRINITY GOD CREATED ADAM AND EVE.

#13. THERE WAS <u>NO SUCH THING AS A TRINITY GOD</u> RESTED ON THE SEVENTH DAY AFTER CREATION.

#14. GOD <u>DID NOT</u> HAVE A BEGOTTEN SON IN HEAVEN CALLED, JESUS, BEFORE THE ANGELS WERE CREATED.

....

....

....

....

<u>PLEASE, TRY AND UNDERSTAND THE FOURTEEN POINTS LISTED ABOVE, TO AVOID MISINTERPRETING GENESIS 1:26.</u>

<u>THE TRINITY GOD THEORY IS ANTI-CHRIST.</u>

....

....

....

....

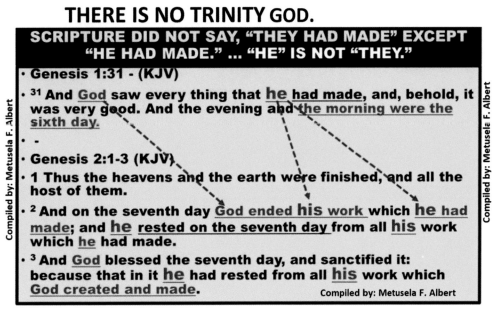

THERE IS NO TRINITY GOD.

SCRIPTURE DID NOT SAY, "THEY HAD MADE" EXCEPT "HE HAD MADE." ... "HE" IS NOT "THEY."

- Genesis 1:31 - (KJV)
- 31 And God saw every thing that he had made, and, behold, it was very good. And the evening and the morning were the sixth day.
- -
- Genesis 2:1-3 (KJV)
- 1 Thus the heavens and the earth were finished, and all the host of them.
- 2 And on the seventh day God ended his work which he had made; and he rested on the seventh day from all his work which he had made.
- 3 And God blessed the seventh day, and sanctified it: because that in it he had rested from all his work which God created and made.

Compiled by: Metusela F. Albert

Compiled by: Metusela F. Albert

....
....
....
....

PLEASE READ THE SINGULAR PRONOUNS .... THIS IS <u>NOT</u> A TRINITY GOD.
• Genesis 1:27 – So <u>GOD</u> created man in <u>HIS</u> own image, in the image of <u>GOD</u> created <u>HE</u> him; male and female created <u>HE</u> them."
• Genesis 1:31 – And <u>GOD</u> saw everything that <u>HE</u> had made, and , behold, it was very good. And the evening and the morning were<u>the sixth day</u>.
• Genesis 2:1 – Thus the heavens and the earth were finished, and all the host of them.
• Genesis 2:2 – And on <u>the seventh day</u> <u>GOD</u> ended <u>HIS</u> work which <u>HE</u> had made, and <u>HE</u> rested on the seventh day from all <u>HIS</u> work which <u>HE</u> had made.
• Genesis 2:3 – And <u>GOD</u> blessed the seventh day and sanctified it because that in it <u>HE</u> had rested from all <u>HIS</u> work which <u>GOD</u> created and made.

JESUS, WHO WAS THE LORD OF THE SABBATH DAY, WAS NOT A TRINITY GOD.

....
....
....
....

THE GOD WHO SPOKE TO ADAM AND EVE AFTER THEIR FALL WAS NOT A TRINITY GOD.

LET'S READ GENESIS 3:8-11.

THE GOD WHO SPOKE TO ADAM AND EVE WAS NOT A TRINITY GOD. . . . READ GENESIS 3:8 -11.

- [8] And they heard the voice of the LORD God walking in the garden in the cool of the day: and Adam and his wife hid themselves from the presence of the LORD God amongst the trees of the garden.

- [9] And the LORD God called unto Adam, and said unto him, Where art thou?

- [10] And he said, I heard thy voice in the garden, and I was afraid, because I was naked; and I hid myself.

- [11] And he said, Who told thee that thou wast naked? Hast thou eaten of the tree, whereof I commanded thee that thou shouldest not eat?

Compiled by: Metusela F. Albert.

CHAPTER 6

THE GOD OF NOAH WAS <u>NOT</u> A TRINITY GOD. READ GENESIS 6.

1 And it came to pass, when men began to multiply on the face of the earth, and daughters were born unto them,

² That the sons of God saw the daughters of men that they were fair; and they took them wives of all which they chose.

³ And <u>the Lord said</u>, <u>My spirit</u> shall not always strive with man, for that he also is flesh: yet his days shall be an hundred and twenty years.

⁴ There were giants in the earth in those days; and also after that, when the sons of God came in unto the daughters of men, and they bare children to them, the same became mighty men which were of old, men of renown.

⁵ And <u>God</u> saw that the wickedness of man was great in the earth, and that every imagination of the thoughts of his heart was only evil continually.

⁶ And it repented <u>the Lord that he</u> had made man on the earth, and it grieved <u>him</u> at <u>his</u> heart.

⁷ And <u>the Lord said, I will destroy man whom I have created</u> from the face of the earth; both man, and beast, and the creeping thing, and the fowls of the air; <u>for it repenteth me that I have made them</u>.

⁸ But Noah found grace in the eyes of <u>the Lord</u>.

⁹ These are the generations of Noah: Noah was a just man and perfect in his generations, and <u>Noah walked with God</u>.

¹⁰ And Noah begat three sons, Shem, Ham, and Japheth.

¹¹ The earth also was corrupt before <u>God,</u> and the earth was filled with violence.

¹² And <u>God</u> looked upon the earth, and, behold, it was corrupt; for all flesh had corrupted his way upon the earth.

¹³ And <u>God</u> said unto Noah, The end of all flesh is come before <u>me;</u> for the earth is filled with violence through them; and, behold, <u>I will destroy them</u> with the earth.

¹⁴ Make thee an ark of gopher wood; rooms shalt thou make in the ark, and shalt pitch it within and without with pitch.

¹⁵ And this is the fashion which thou shalt make it of: The length of the ark shall be three hundred cubits, the breadth of it fifty cubits, and the height of it thirty cubits.

¹⁶ A window shalt thou make to the ark, and in a cubit shalt thou finish it above; and the door of the ark shalt thou set in the side thereof; with lower, second, and third stories shalt thou make it.

¹⁷ And, <u>behold, I, even I,</u> do bring a flood of waters upon the earth, to destroy all flesh, wherein is the breath of life, from under heaven; and every thing that is in the earth shall die.

¹⁸ <u>But with thee will I establish my covenant</u>; and thou shalt come into the ark, thou, and thy sons, and thy wife, and thy sons' wives with thee.

¹⁹ And of every living thing of all flesh, two of sort shalt thou every bring into the ark, to keep them alive with thee; they shall be male and female.

20 Of fowls after their kind, and of cattle after their kind, of every creeping thing of the earth after his kind, two of every sort shall come unto thee, to keep them alive.

21 And take thou unto thee of all food that is eaten, and thou shalt gather it to thee; and it shall be for food for thee, and for them.

22 Thus did Noah; according to all that God commanded him, so did he.

....
....
....
....

**THE GOD OF NOAH WAS NOT A TRINITY GOD.
. . . TRY AND READ THE SINGULAR PRONOUNS. . .**

- **READ GENESIS 6:6-7.**

- **6 And it repented the Lord that he had made man on the earth, and it grieved him at his heart.**

- **7 And the Lord said, I will destroy man whom I have created from the face of the earth; both man, and beast, and the creeping thing, and the fowls of the air; for it repenteth me that I have made them.**

Compiled by: Metusela F. Albert.

PLEASE, READ THE "SINGULAR PRONOUNS ABOUT GOD" IN GENESIS CHAPTER 6, AS POSTED ABOVE FOR YOUR INFORMATION.

IN FACT, THE GOD WHO SPOKE TO NOAH WAS THE CREATOR, THE ELOHIM, WHO CREATED HEAVEN

AND EARTH, WHO SPOKE TO ADAM AND EVE AT THE GARDEN OF EDEN.

ELOHIM WAS <u>NOT</u> A TRINITY GOD.

....

....

....

....

CHAPTER 7

THE GOD OF ABRAHAM WAS NOT A TRINITY GOD.

LET'S READ - GENESIS 12:1-3.

THE GOD OF ABRAHAM WAS NOT A TRINITY GOD

- Genesis 12:1-3.(King James Version).

- 1. Now **the LORD** had said unto Abram, "Get thee out of thy country, and from thy kindred and from thy father's house, unto a land that **I** will show thee.

- ² And **I** will make of thee a great nation, and **I** will bless thee and make thy name great; and thou shalt be a blessing.

- ³ And **I** will bless them that bless thee, and curse him that curseth thee; and in thee shall all families of the earth be blessed."

DID YOU NOTICE THAT THE PRONOUN "I" WAS MENTIONED FOUR (4) TIMES? . . . . NOT "WE"

Compiled by: Metusela F. Albert

FURTHER EVIDENCE (PROOF) THAT THE GOD OF ABRAHAM AND THE CHILDREN OF ISRAEL WAS NOT A TRINITY GOD.

READ WHAT JESUS SAID IN THE NEW TESTAMENT TO THE JEWISH UNBELIEVERS AS RECORDED IN THE BOOK OF

JOHN AND THE BOOK OF LUKE. A POWERPOINT SLIDE IS PROVIDED BELOW TO HIGHLIGHT THE POINT.

JESUS WAS THE GOD (YAHWEH / JEHOVAH) OF ABRAHAM AND THE PROPHETS, IN THE OLD TESTAMENT.

1

JESUS said, "Search the Scriptures, for in them ye think you have eternal life; and it is they which testify of ME." John 5:39.

2

• JESUS said, "For had ye believed Moses, ye would have believed Me, for he wrote of Me." John 5:46.

3

• LUKE 24:25-27

25 Then JESUS said unto them, "O fools, and slow of heart to believe all that the prophets have spoken!

26 Ought not Christ to have suffered these things and to enter into His glory?"

27 And beginning with Moses and all the prophets, He expounded unto them in all the Scriptures the things concerning Himself."   Compiled by: Metusela F. Albert.

THE TORAH –
MOSES WROTE THESE FIVE BOOKS LISTED BELOW.

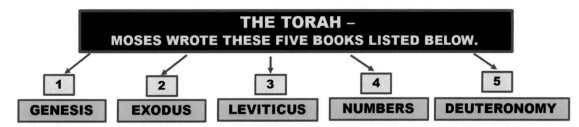

1	2	3	4	5
GENESIS	EXODUS	LEVITICUS	NUMBERS	DEUTERONOMY

JESUS said to the unbelieving Jews, "Had ye believed Moses, ye would have believed Me; for he wrote about Me." (John 5:46).

Genesis 1:1 – "In the beginning God created the heaven and the earth."

NOTE: The "God" (Elohim / Yahweh / Jehovah) that you read in those five Books was JESUS.
It was JESUS who created heaven and earth in six days and rested on the seventh day – (Genesis 1:1-31; 2:1-3).
HE was not the Son of God when he created heaven and earth.
JESUS was the GOD of Abraham who later became the Son of God by incarnation through Mary at Bethlehem – (Genesis 12:1-3; John 8:56-58; Luke 1:35).

Compiled by: Metusela F. Albert

....

....

....

....

CHAPTER 8

JESUS WAS THE GOD CALLED "I AM THAT I AM."

Read - EXODUS 3:13-14. John 5:39, 46; 8:56-58.

THE GOD OF ABRAHAM WAS NOT A TRINITY GOD

- Genesis 12:1-3.(King James Version).

- 1. Now **the LORD** had said unto Abram, "Get thee out of thy country, and from thy kindred and from thy father's house, unto a land that I will show thee.

- 2 And I will make of thee a great nation, and I will bless thee and make thy name great; and thou shalt be a blessing.

- 3 And I will bless them that bless thee, and curse him that curseth thee; and in thee shall all families of the earth be blessed."

DID YOU NOTICE THAT THE PRONOUN "I" WAS MENTIONED FOUR (4) TIMES? . . . . NOT "WE"

Compiled by: Metusela F. Albert

....
....
....
....

THE GOD OF ABRAHAM DID NOT HAVE A SON IN HEAVEN CALLED - JESUS.

NOTE: JESUS WAS THE GOD OF ABRAHAM WHO HUMBLY TOOK HUMAN FLESH THROUGH MARY AT BETHLEHEM.

THIS WAS THE INCARNATION PROCESS.

Read - Genesis 1:1-31; 2:1-3; Exodus 3:13-14;6:1-3; Isaiah 43:10-11; 44:6, 24; 49:16; John 5:39, 46; 8:56-58; Revelation 21:6-7.

....
....
....
....

JESUS WAS THE GOD OF KING DAVID. HE was the ELOHIM who created heaven and earth. HE was not a Trinity GOD. Let's read it in Psalm 95:5-8 and 90:2.

THE GOD WHO CREATED HEAVEN AND EARTH-

- Psalm 95:5 – The sea is His, and He made it: and His hands formed the dray land.
- Psalm 95:6 – O come, let us worship and bow down: let us kneel before the LORD our MAKER.
- Psalm 95:7 – For He is our GOD; and we are the people of His pasture, and the sheep of His hand. To-day if ye will hear His voice,
- Psalm 95:8 - Harden not your heart, ...

- Psalm 90:2 – "Before the mountains were brought forth, or ever thou hadst formed the earth and the world, even from everlasting to everlasting thou art GOD."

....
....
....
....

It was "ELOHIM" who took Human Flesh through Mary at Bethlehem by the INCARNATION process, AND BECAME THE SON OF GOD, to die at calvary as our Sin Bearer / Savior. HIS NAME IS – "JESUS".

READ – Genesis 1:1-31; 2:1-3; Exodus 3:13-14; 6:1-3; Isaiah 43:10-11; 44:6, 24; 49:16; John 5:39, 46; 8:56-58; Revelation 21:6-7.

Compiled by: Metusela F. Albert.

....
....
....
....

CHAPTER 9

JESUS WAS THE GOD CALLED – "THE FIRST AND THE LAST". READ - ISAIAH 43:10-11; 44:6, 24; REVELATION 21:5-7.

THE ELOHIM WHO CREATED HEAVEN AND EARTH, SPOKE TO PROPHET ISAIAH AND PROPHESIED ABOUT HIS CRUCIFIXION – Isaiah 49:16. The POWERPOINT SLIDE shown below shows that Prophet Isaiah lived around 730 B.C.

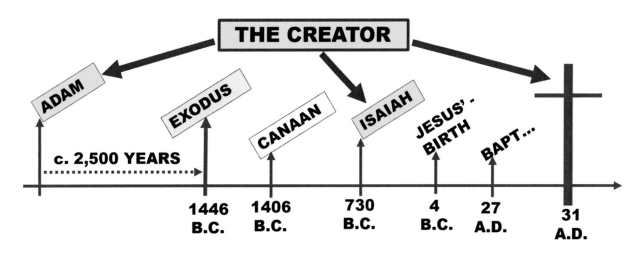

ISAIAH 49:16 – "BEHOLD, I HAVE GRAVEN THEE UPON THE PALMS OF MY HANDS; THY WALLS ARE CONTINUALLY BEFORE ME."

....
....
....
....

CHAPTER 10

JESUS WAS THE ALPHA AND OMEGA. REVELATION 21:5-7.

FIRST, LET'S READ - REVELATION 14:6.

THERE IS NO SUCH THING AS A TRINITY GOD.

- Revelation 14:6 – The angel says, "Fear **GOD** and give glory to **Him**; for the hour of **His** judgment is come."

THIS GOD IN HEAVEN IS **NOT** A TRINITY GOD.

READ THE SINGULAR MALE GENDER PRONOUN AND LEARN THE TRUTH.

Compiled by: Metusela F. Albert.

....
....
....
....

- **JESUS WAS THE GOD (ELOHIM / YAHWEH / JEHOVAH) WHO WROTE THE TEN COMMANDMENTS.**
-
- **Scripture:**
-
- **Exodus 20:1-3**
- **1. And <u>God</u> spake all these words, saying,**

- **² <u>I am the LORD thy God</u>, <u>which have brought thee out of the land of Egypt, out of the house of bondage.</u>**

- **³ Thou shalt have no other gods before <u>me.</u>**

THIS WAS NOT A TRINITY GOD. . . Look at the Singular PRONOUN.

....

....

....

....

ONE MORE TIME. LET'S READ REVELATION 21:5-7 TO ENSURE THAT WE UNDERSTAND THE GOD THAT IS SITTING ON THE THRONE.

PAUL CONTADICTED REVELATION 21:5-7, WHEN HE WROTE IN HEBREWS 12:2, THAT JESUS ASCENDED TO HEAVEN AND SAT ON THE RIGHT HAND OF GOD ON THE THRONE. ACCORDING TO PAUL, GOD THE FATHER AND JESUS WERE TWO DISTINCT BEINGS ON THE THRONE.

- **Revelation 21:5-7 - King James Version**

- **⁵ And he that sat upon the throne said,**

- **Behold, I make all things new. And he said unto me, Write: for these words are true and faithful.**

- **⁶ And he said unto me, It is done. I am Alpha and Omega, the beginning and the end. I will give unto him that is athirst of the fountain of the water of life freely.**

- **⁷ He that overcometh shall inherit all things; and I will be his God, and he shall be my son.**

Compiled by: Metusela F. Albert.

....
....
....
....

"ELOHIM"
CREATED HEAVEN AND EARTH.

JESUS WAS THE "ELOHIM" WHO CREATED HEAVEN AND EARTH.

THEREFORE, JESUS WHO WAS "ELOHIM,"
DID NOT HAVE A BEGOTTEN SON CALLED - JESUS.

....
....
....
....

CHAPTER 11

BIBLICAL TIMELINE OF EVENTS FROM CREATION TIME. CHURCH HISTORY.

....
....
....
....

The events from Genesis to the time of JESUS and after His Crucifixion, is very important for us to know because it helps us to understand <u>the bigger picture of GOD</u> revealing himself to us in writing. It also reveals the <u>nearness of the return of JESUS</u>, and the hereafter – the Millennium, the city JERUSALEM, and the renewal of our planet earth and life eternal with GOD.

The stories that we read in the Bible refer to <u>a particular time</u>, <u>not just bedtime stories</u>.

Therefore, check out the Biblical Events timeline. Not every event is fitted inside the timeline I compiled because of the shortness of space. Any other Biblical event that you think is important, the timeline is given and you can pinpoint the place in the given timeline.

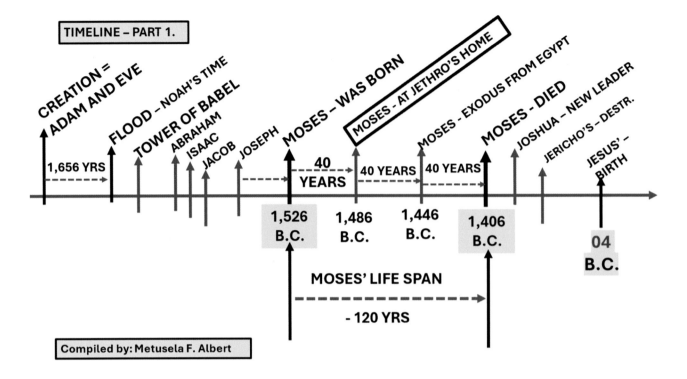

TIMELINE – PART 1.

CREATION = ADAM AND EVE

FLOOD – NOAH'S TIME

TOWER OF BABEL

ABRAHAM

ISAAC

JACOB

JOSEPH

MOSES – WAS BORN

MOSES - AT JETHRO'S HOME

MOSES - EXODUS FROM EGYPT

MOSES - DIED

JOSHUA – NEW LEADER

JERICHO'S – DESTR.

JESUS' – BIRTH

1,656 YRS

40 YEARS   40 YEARS   40 YEARS

1,526 B.C.

1,486 B.C.

1,446 B.C.

1,406 B.C.

04 B.C.

MOSES' LIFE SPAN - 120 YRS

Compiled by: Metusela F. Albert

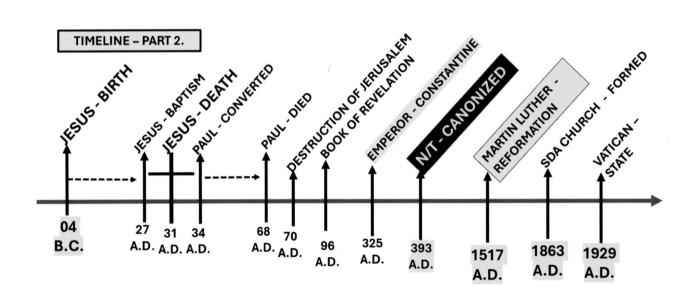

TIMELINE – PART 2.

JESUS - BIRTH

JESUS - BAPTISM

JESUS - DEATH

PAUL - CONVERTED

PAUL - DIED

DESTRUCTION OF JERUSALEM

BOOK OF REVELATION

EMPEROR - CONSTANTINE

N/T - CANONIZED

MARTIN LUTHER - REFORMATION

SDA CHURCH - FORMED

VATICAN - STATE

04 B.C.

27 A.D.

31 A.D.

34 A.D.

68 A.D.

70 A.D.

96 A.D.

325 A.D.

393 A.D.

1517 A.D.

1863 A.D.

1929 A.D.

Compiled by: Metusela F. Albert.

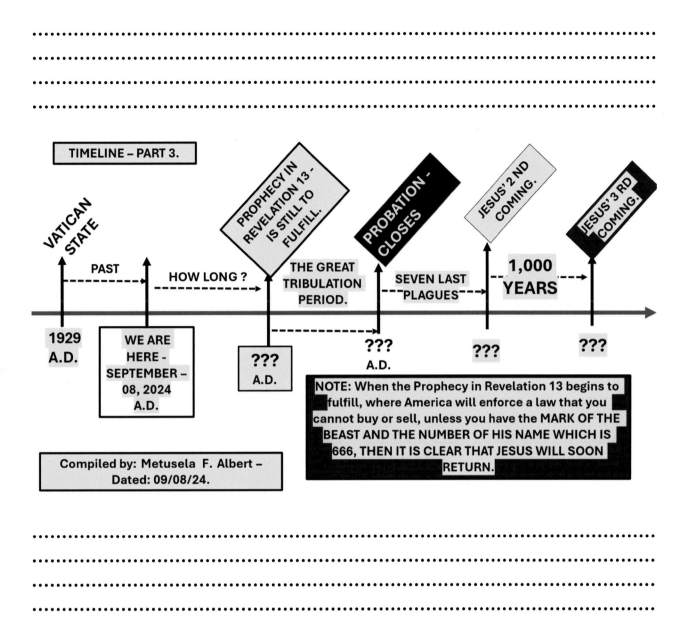

I hope these <u>three PowerPoint Slides</u> regarding the PAST Biblical Events and the FUTURE Events, are of help to you about the <u>nearness</u> of JESUS' 2ND COMING. His second coming is <u>not</u> soon until those who are alive during the time the Prophecy in Revelation 13, begins to fulfill. This is the Prophecy that America will enforce a <u>NATIONAL LAW</u> where you <u>cannot buy or sell,</u> unless you have <u>the Mark of the Beast, and the number of his name, which is 666 – (Revelation 13:17-18). That will mark the beginning of the Great Tribulation era. And will be followed by the seven last plagues, then</u>

the return of JESUS. The return of JESUS will mark the beginning of the MILLENNIUM (1,000 Years). Check the TIMELINE CHART.

....

....

....

....

CHAPTER 12

GOD DID NOT HAVE A BEGOTTEN SON, IN HEAVEN.

After seriously discussing the previous Chapters about JESUS, now we can make the serious Conclusion, which is the bottom-line.

When you come to a good understanding that JESUS was, and is, the only GOD in heaven, common-sense would tell you that JESUS DID NOT SEND A SON CALLED JESUS to die at Calvary. True? Of Course! . . . THINK! THINK! THINK!

A good sound minded person cannot fail to use common-sense and logic that JESUS, is the only GOD in heaven. Therefore, the Trinity GOD theory is wrong and Satanic. The Trinity GOD teaching is Anti-Christ because it tries to reduce JESUS from being the only everlasting GOD without a beginning, to a creature, either created by the Father or born by the Father in heaven.

"IF" JESUS was born by the Father in heaven, then it is promoting the notion that JESUS was born twice; born in heaven and born the second time by Mary at Bethlehem. THIS IS INSANE AND RIDICULUS.

We as Christians must confront and condemn aggressively the false Trinity GOD theory because our gospel about GOD'S LOVE should be based on the fact that JESUS was, and is, our only GOD who came down and became a human being like us and died at Calvary to be mankind's Sin Bearer / Savior. THIS SHOULD BE OUR GOSPEL.

Just because most Churches failed to understand it, that does not make the truth to be wrong because we are just a minority of people who believed it. Remember, during the time of the flood, only eight people believed the truth about the coming flood, entered the ARK, and got saved. The vast majority of the people did not believe what Noah was telling them about the truth of a flood.

Read ISAIAH 43:10-11. There was no GOD before him and after him.

....
....
....
....

DID YOU NOT KNOW YET????

- JOHN 1:1-3; John 3:16, and 1 JOHN 5:7, ARE ALL WRONG.
- JOHN CONTRADICTED WHAT GOD (JESUS) SAID ABOUT HIMSELF, IN ISAIAH 43:10-11; 44:6, 24; 49:16.
- There was no such thing as a Trinity GOD nor a Duality GOD.
- And there was no such thing as the GOD of Abraham gave birth to a begotten Son in heaven, prior to the existence of Lucifer and the angels.

Compiled by: Metusela F. Albert

....
....
....
....

- **Revelation 21:5-7 - King James Version**

- **5 And he that sat upon the throne said, Behold, I make all things new. And he said unto me, Write: for these words are true and faithful.**

- **6 And he said unto me, It is done. I am Alpha and Omega, the beginning and the end. I will give unto him that is athirst of the fountain of the water of life freely.**

- **7 He that overcometh shall inherit all things; and I will be his God, and he shall be my son.**

Compiled by: Metusela F. Albert.

ONE MORE POINT THAT NEEDS TO BE CLARIFIED. WHO WAS THE HOLY SPIRIT?

The Holy Spirit was the Spirit of GOD – Genesis 1:1-3. Since we have proven that JESUS was, and is, <u>the Only GOD</u> in heaven, <u>therefore, the Holy Spirit was the Spirit of JESUS</u>. When JESUS abides in you, the Holy Spirit abides in you because the Holy Spirit is the Spirit of JESUS.

The Holy Spirit is <u>not</u> a person nor a third person. JESUS is the person. The Holy Spirit is <u>not</u> the person.

//
//
//
//

THE TRUTH IS:

JESUS, WHO WAS THE FATHER, TOOK HUMAN FLESH BY INCARNATION THROUGH MARY AT BETHLEHEM, AND BECAME THE SON. HE VOLUNTARILY DIED AT CALVARY, TO PAY FOR THE PENALTY OF SIN, AS IF HE WAS A SINNER. THIS IS THE MOST AMAZING LOVE OF GOD.

JESUS, WHO WAS GOD THE FATHER <u>BECAME THE SON</u> BY THE INCARNATION PROCESS THROUGH MARY AT BETHLEHEM.

GOD DID <u>NOT</u> SEND A SON. GOD DID <u>NOT</u> HAVE A BEGOTTEN SON. JESUS WAS THE ONLY GOD FROM ETERNITY.

....
....
....
....

> **"ELOHIM" CREATED HEAVEN AND EARTH.**
>
> ↓
>
> **JESUS WAS THE "ELOHIM" WHO CREATED HEAVEN AND EARTH.**
>
> ↓
>
> **THEREFORE, JESUS WHO WAS "ELOHIM," DID NOT HAVE A BEGOTTEN SON CALLED - JESUS.**

....
....
....
....

CHAPTER 13

THE "BORN TWICE THEORY" BY <u>JOHN</u> (JOHN 3:16).

Let's Read - John 3:16.

"For <u>God</u> so loved the world, <u>that he gave his only begotten Son</u>, that whosoever believeth in <u>him</u> should <u>not</u> perish, but have everlasting life".

John 3:16, is the most memorized text in every generation. This is the text that Christianity claims to prove the amazing love of GOD, for thousands of years, and still is, today.

This Book is going to challenge us to rethink of the true love of GOD and reinterpret Scripture in the Context that has not been explained well. What is it? <u>GOD did not send a Begotten Son to die at Calvary.</u> Really? Of course! Stay tuned and follow me well.

....
....
....
....

CRUCIAL POINT: GOD became human flesh by <u>the INCARNATION process</u> through Mary at Bethlehem and became the Son of GOD.

....
....
....
....

<u>ACCORDING to John 3:16, this was what it advocated</u>: -

1. That GOD had a begotten Son in heaven called – "JESUS," <u>before</u> the angels existed.
2. That GOD <u>sent</u> his only begotten Son (JESUS), to die at Calvary as the Sin Bearer, Savior of mankind.
3. That GOD the Father and his Son, were <u>TWO DISTINCT DIVINE BEINGS</u>.
4. That JESUS was <u>first,</u> born by the Father in heaven, and born <u>the second time</u> through Mary at Bethlehem.
5. In other words, "<u>JESUS WAS BORN TWICE</u>."
6. The "<u>BORN TWICE</u>" theory was instigated by John in John 3:16, which contradicted Genesis 1:1 and Isaiah 43:10-11.

....
....
....
....

<u>NOTE</u>: THE BORN TWICE THEORY IS A SATANIC DOCTRINE. IT IS ANTI-CHRIST.

HOW?

 # 1. It demoted JESUS, who was the <u>only GOD</u> that is sitting on the THRONE, to a creature with a beginning. It made JESUS to be <u>not</u> the Alpha and Omega.

 # 2. It contradicted what GOD said to Prophet Isaiah in Isaiah 43:10-11, that <u>HE alone is GOD; none before him, and none after him.</u>

....
....
....
....

NOTE: IF you believe that John 3:16 is correct, thus you are believing in <u>the "BORN TWICE" theory</u>, unconsciously. This probably must have shocked you, but that is the reality.

Why do you think I wrote this Book for? For us to unlearn things that were <u>not</u> correct and re-educate ourselves and hold on to what is Biblical and logical. Try and understand Isaiah 43:10-11, I posted as the Scripture Reading at the very beginning of this Book.

THE THEOLOGICAL SEMINARIES NEED TO REVAMP A NEW CURRICULUM TO TEACH PASTORS OF THE REAL GOSPEL THAT <u>JESUS WAS THE ELOHIM WHO</u>

CREATED HEAVEN AND EARTH IN SIX DAYS AND RESTED ON THE SEVENTH DAY.

....

....

....

....

CHAPTER 14

WHO WAS SITTING ON THE THRONE? JESUS, <u>THE LORD GOD ALMIGHTY.</u>

Read Revelation 4:8-11.

⁸ And the four beasts had each of them six wings about him; and they were full of eyes within: and they rest not day and night, <u>saying, Holy, holy, holy, Lord God Almighty, which was, and is, and is to come.</u>

⁹ And when those beasts give glory and honour and thanks <u>to him that sat on the throne, who liveth for ever and ever,</u>

¹⁰ The four and twenty elders fall down <u>before him that sat on the throne, and worship him that liveth for ever and ever, and cast their crowns before the throne, saying,</u>

¹¹ <u>Thou art worthy, O Lord, to receive glory and honour and power: for thou hast created all things, and for thy pleasure they are and were created.</u>

....

....

....

....

A. SEVEN OUTSTANDING POINTS NEED TO BE CAREFULLY NOTED ABOUT THE ONE SITTING ON THE THRONE:

1. HE WAS THE LORD GOD ALMIGHTY, WHICH WAS, AND IS, AND IS TO COME – v. 8.

2. HE LIVETH FOR EVER AND EVER – v. 9 and v. 10.

3. HE WAS THE CREATOR – v.11.

4. ONLY ONE WAS SEEN BY JOHN, TO BE SITTING ON THE THRONE – v. 10 and v. 11.

5. NO SON OF GOD WAS SEEN TO BE SITTING ON THE RIGHT HAND OF THE FATHER. (Paul who wrote Hebrews 12:2. Contradicted this Text).

6. WORSHIP IS DUE TO ONLY ONE DIVINE BEING, THE CREATOR OF HEAVEN AND EARTH. We are not to worship three persons or a Trinity GOD.

7. NO THREE PERSONS NAMED – THE FATHER, THE SON, THE HOLY SPIRIT, WERE SEEN AS SITTING ON THE THRONE.

B. WHO FITS PERFECTLY TO THOSE SEVEN (7) POINTS LISTED ABOVE, AS TAKEN FROM REVELATION CHAPTER 4:1-11?

- JESUS, HE WAS THE LORD GOD ALMIGHTY OF ABRAHAM, MOSES, AND THE PROPHETS.

- JESUS, WHO CAME IN <u>HUMAN FLESH</u>, AND DIED AT CALVARY. HE RESURRECTED AND LIVETH FOREVER AND EVER. HE WAS THE RESURRECTION AND THE LIFE.

- JESUS, WHO WAS THE <u>ELOHIM</u> WHO CREATED HEAVEN AND EARTH IN SIX DAYS AND RESTED ON THE SEVENTH DAY.

- JESUS, WORSHIP IS DUE TO HIM – John 4:24-27; Revelation 14:6-7; 21:5-7.

- JESUS, HE WAS <u>NOT</u> A TRINITY GOD.

....
....
....
....

A VERY CRUCIAL POINT: THERE WAS NO "SON OF GOD," SEEN BY JOHN, AS SITTING ON THE THRONE OR SITTING ON THE RIGHT-HAND OF GOD, IN HEAVEN.

NOTE: PROFESSED CHRISTIANS AND MAINLINE DENOMINATIONS NEED TO BE ENLIGHTENED FURTHER ON THIS SUBJECT, TO HAVE A <u>TRUE GOSPEL</u> ABOUT JESUS, THE ONLY ONE WHO SITS ON THE THRONE.

<u>A REVIVAL AND REFORMATION IS NEEDED ON THIS SUBJECT BEFORE THE SECOND COMING OF JESUS.</u>

THE THIRD ANGEL'S MESSAGE OF REVELATION 14:6, HAS TO BE VERY <u>PRECISE</u> AND <u>CLEAR, IN REGARD TO THE ONE SITING ON THE THRONE</u>.

THE GOD WHO REVEALED HIMSELF TO JOHN ON THE ISLAND OF PATMOS WAS JESUS - . . . . HE WAS NOT A TRINITY GOD. HE WAS THE ALPHA AND OMEGA – Revelation 21:6-7.

• Revelation 14:6 – The angel says, "Fear <u>GOD</u> and give glory to <u>Him</u>; for the hour of <u>His</u> judgment is come."

THIS GOD IN HEAVEN IS <u>NOT</u> A TRINITY GOD.

READ THE SINGULAR MALE GENDER PRONOUN AND LEARN THE TRUTH.

Compiled by: Metusela F. Albert.

CONCLUSION

Dear Reader, NOW, you should have noticed the misinterpretation of Genesis 1:26, to justify a Trinity GOD theory. In fact, the Trinity GOD theory is ANTI-CHRIST. It degraded JESUS from being our only GOD, sitting on the THRONE; to a creature with a beginning and an ending, which makes JESUS, not the ALPHA AND OMEGA, not the FIRST AND THE LAST, not the GREAT I AM, not JEHOVAH, not ELOHIM, who created heaven and earth in six days and rested on the seventh day.

This Book is focused on helping the reader to learn HOW to Read and Interpret Scripture, in the CONTEXT, and in a CHRONOLOGICAL Order, beginning from Genesis Chapter 1:1-31; 2:1-3.

This Book also condemns the False Interpretation of Genesis 1:26 by most Churches and their Pastors, to justify the Trinity GOD theory.

Probably, you who believed in the Trinity GOD theory, may have not realized yet that your doctrine is ANTI-CHRIST. You are against CHRIST in a very subtle way. Your subconscious mind has not realized it yet. And that is why this Book is written to wake your mind up from your your sleeping mode.

It is like your phone call that the operator on the other side puts it <u>on hold</u> for a while, but your waiting time exceeds 15 minutes. Now, your many years of waiting to have this subject clarified, is over. Give the Almighty GOD, the glory and the praise.

Please, share this true Gospel about JESUS with your friends and Churches.

THE TRINITY GOD THEORY IS ANTI-CHRIST.

- The <u>Trinity</u> GOD theory promotes the idea that JESUS cannot be GOD by himself; for he must be added to another Two Divine Beings; the Father and the Holy Spirit, to make one GOD.
- They call it – "THREE IN ONE."
- 1 + 1 + 1 = 1 GOD.
- THE TRINITY GOD THEORY IS ANTI-CHRIST.

Compiled by: Metuela F. Albert.

Thank you for taking the time to purchase and read this Book with an open mind.

If you require further reading on this subject, please consider getting one of these three Books, I wrote about JESUS.

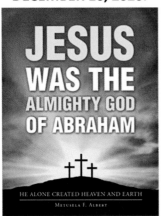
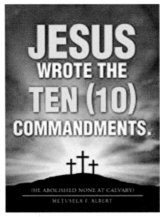

NOTE: JESUS WAS THE ALMIGHTY GOD (JEHOVAH / YAHWEH) OF ABRAHAM, THE FATHER, WHO BECAME THE SON OF GOD, THROUGH MARY AT BETHLEHEM.

HE WAS NOT THE SON OF ABRAHAM'S GOD.

HERE, GET THIS: THE GOD OF ABRAHAM DID NOT HAVE A BEGOTTEN SON CALLED - JESUS.

IF YOU DID NOT UNDERSTAND THE PRONOUNS ("HE") THAT WERE USED THREE TIMES, IN GENESIS 1:5, 10, 16, HENCE, YOU WOULD NOT HAVE UNDERSTOOD THIS TRUTH ABOUT JESUS, THE ELOHIM, WHO CREATED HEAVEN AND EARTH, WHO BECAME THE SON OF GOD, BY THE INCARNATION PROCESS THROUGH MARY AT BETHLEHEM.

WE MUST EVALUATE THE NEW TESTAMENT BY THE OLD TESTAMENT. ASSESS JOHN 1:1; 3:16, AND COLOSSIANS 1:15-18, BY ISAIAH 43:10-11.

Check my website: www.Jesusthegodofabraham.com. . . . Look for more Books on other controversial subjects that you may have not understood it yet, or may be of interest to you. Thank you.

....
....
....
....

THE TRUTH IS:

JESUS, WHO WAS THE FATHER, TOOK HUMAN FLESH BY INCARNATION THROUGH MARY AT BETHLEHEM, AND BECAME THE SON. HE VOLUNTARILY DIED AT CALVARY, TO PAY FOR THE PENALTY OF SIN, AS IF HE WAS A SINNER. THIS IS THE MOST AMAZING LOVE OF GOD.

GOD THE FATHER BECAME THE SON BY THE INCARNATION PROCESS. GOD DID NOT SEND A SON TO DIE AT CALVARY. IN FACT, GOD DID NOT HAVE A

BEGOTTEN SON, IN HEAVEN, BEFORE THE ANGELS EXISTED.

> **IF CHRISTIANITY HAD UNDERSTOOD WHAT GOD SAID TO PROPHET ISAIAH IN CHAPTER 43:10-11, HENCE, THEY WOULD NOT HAVE FALLEN INTO THE LIES OF A TRINITY GOD THEORY.**
>
> ....
>
> • **WE MUST CONFRONT, CONDEMN, AND REBUKE, THE FALSE TRINITY GOD THEORY, THAT DECEIVED MILLIONS OF PEOPLE FOR DECADES.**
>
> • **The Trinity GOD concept has <u>demoted</u> JESUS from being a self-existent GOD, to a Son of GOD, with a beginning, born by GOD the FATHER in eternity, before the angels existed.**
>
> Compiled by: Metusela F. Albert

IF you believe in a Trinity GOD, then you are transgressing Commandments # 1 and # 2, in the Ten Commandments. <u>You have an idol god</u>. Think about it, seriously.

IF you believe in John 1:1, then you believe in <u>the DUALITY GOD</u> theory, which is wrong. This text contradicted Isaiah 43:10-11.

JOHN 1:1, WAS WRONG.

"With" is the preposition.

- **Greek NT: John Chapter 1.1**
- **ἐν ἀρχῇ ἦν ὁ *λόγος*, καὶ ὁ *λόγος* ἦν πρὸς τὸν θεόν, καὶ θεὸς ἦν ὁ λόγος.**

- **In the beginning was the Word, and the Word was with God, and the Word was God.**
-
- **EXPLANATION-**
- **According to John, the Word which was JESUS, was with God in the beginning.**
- **And the Word was also God.**
- **According to John, there were TWO Gods in the beginning. The God of**
- **Abraham and the Word, which was JESUS.**

Most Professed Christians have <u>not</u> understood yet that John 1:1 promoted <u>the "TWO GODS" theory</u> – <u>the DUALITY GOD theory.</u>

It was John who also wrote about <u>the "TRINITY GOD" theory, in 1 John 5:7</u>. Those two theories by John contradicted Genesis 1:1 and Isaiah 43:10-11.

Sadly, today, most Churches failed to notice the contradiction by John, because they failed to understand Isaiah 43:10-11. Here is the thing. You cannot understand the contradiction by John until you first understand Isaiah 43:10-11. I hope you get this point.

Furthermore, if you believed that "GOD had a Begotten Son in heaven (John 3:16)", sad to say, indirectly, you will have to believe that <u>JESUS was born TWICE</u>; born in heaven from eternity by the Father, and born <u>the second time</u> through Mary, at Bethlehem.

You know what? You did <u>not</u> know that you believed in <u>the BORN TWICE theory</u> about JESUS, since you believed that John 3:16 was correct. Think! Think! Think!

....
....
....
....

QUESTIONNAIRE – 21 SIMPLE QUESTIONS TO TEST YOUR UNDERSTANDING.

1. What Scripture in the Book of Isaiah reveals that there was only one GOD; none before him and none after him?

   ....

2. What are the three verses in the Book of Genesis Chapter 1 that reveals, the Singular Pronouns "He" before Genesis 1:26?

   ....

3. Who was the LORD of the Sabbath day?

   ....

4. Who was ELOHIM who created heaven and earth in six days and rested on the seventh day

   ....

5. Who was the GOD of Abraham called – "I AM THAT I AM" who spoke to Moses at the burning bush?

....

6. The GOD of Abraham did not have a Begotten Son in heaven called JESUS, because JESUS was the GOD of Abraham. True or

....

7. The GOD of Noah was not a Trinity GOD. . . . True or False?

....

8. The GOD who spoke to Adam and Eve AFTER their Fall, was <u>not </u>a Trinity GOD. . . . True or False?

....

9. JESUS was the GOD called ALPHA and OMEGA, in the Book of Revelation 21:5-7. True or False

....

10. JESUS did not send a Son called JESUS to die at Calvary. True or False?

....

11. JESUS was the Father of the children of Israel who took human flesh and became the Son of GOD. True or False

....

12. There was no such thing as a Trinity GOD. True or False?

....

13. John 1:1 promoted the <u>DUALITY GOD</u> theory. True or False?

....

14. 1 John 5:7 promoted the **TRINITY GOD** theory. True or False?

     ....

15. In Colossians 1:15-18, Paul, wrote that JESUS was the **first-born** of all creatures. According to Paul, Jesus was born by God the Father in heaven and born the second time through Mary at Bethlehem. This is **the Born Twice theory**. This concept demoted Jesus to a creature with a beginning. We should condemn this theory by Paul. True or False?

     ....

16. Paul did **not** know that Jesus was the GOD of Abraham who came in human flesh, to die at Calvary. True or False?

     ....

17. The return of Jesus is **not** soon till the Prophecy in Revelation 13, begins to fulfill. True or False?

     ....

18. The 144,000 refer to **the righteous who are ALIVE,** at the time of JESUS' second coming. True or False?

     ....

19. The second coming of JESUS will mark the beginning of **the Millennium**. True or False?

     ....

20. Jesus is the Alpha and Omega. He is **not** a Trinity God. Revelation 21:5-7. True or False?

     ....

21. THE <u>BORN TWICE THEORY</u> was advocated by John, in John 3:16.
   True or False

....

....
....
....
....

– THE END –

....
....
....
....

THIS <u>PAGE</u> IS FOR YOUR INFORMATION.

Your <u>Name</u>:

....

The <u>Date</u> you Purchased this Book:

....

The <u>Price</u> you paid for the Book:

....

<u>Where</u> did you buy this Book from:

....

Author's email contact. <u>Metusela_albert@yahoo.com</u>

....

THIS IS THE AUTHOR'S 14TH BOOK.

<u>Have you read any other Books written by the Author?</u>

....

The Author would like to hear from you
about your questions for more clarification.
Contact him through email.

The Author is <u>not</u> recommending that you
join a particular denomination.

I, as the Author, is recommending that you join yourself to **JESUS CHRIST** daily.

JESUS CHRIST, IS YOUR SAVIOR. NO DENOMINATION IS YOUR SAVIOR. BELONGING TO A DENOMINATION DOES **NOT** GUARANTEE YOU OF EVERLASTING LIFE.

FELLOWSHIPPING WITH OTHERS AT A CHURCH SERVICE - **DOES NOT** GIVE YOU ETERNAL LIFE. IT SURELY HELPS YOU TO GROW IN YOUR FAITH AS YOU HEAR PERSONAL TESTIMONIES BY OTHERS, AND VICE VERSA.

READ PROVERBS 3:5-6.

TRUST JESUS CHRIST IN ALL TIMES.

CONFESS YOUR SINS TO JESUS AT ANY TIME OF THE DAY, FROM WHEREVER YOU ARE.

TAKE CARE. MAY GOD ABANDUNTANTLY BLESS YOUR FAMILY AND MINISTRY.

....
....
....
....

Printed in the United States
by Baker & Taylor Publisher Services